Look DAMN Good!

Look DAMN Good!

10 Simple Ways to Maximize Your Style

At Your Age, With Your Body
and on Your Budget

*To Portea
my new
Best Friend.
From*

JANET CARGILL

First published by AuthorHouse   07/02/2007

ISBN: 9-781-4343-2178-7

Library of Congress Control Number:2007904929

Printed in the United States of America
Bloomington, Indiana

This book is printed on acid-free paper.

Editors—Claire O'Connor and Barbara Noe
Layout and Design—Angelique Devost, Devost Design LLC
Cover photo taken in May 2006 on Spirit Rock at
Laurel Springs Ranch in Santa Barbara, California

authorHOUSE®

AuthorHouse™
1663 Liberty Drive, Suite 200
Bloomington, IN 47403
www.authorhouse.com
Phone: 1-800-839-8640

This book is dedicated to my parents Leslie and
Mary Gaskell, also known as the handsome
Mr. Leslie of Westfield and his beautiful wife, Suzanne.

Acknowledgments

With love and gratitude to my husband and best friend, Bruce, and to our creative and amazing children: Jennifer, Elizabeth, Bruce, Amy, Peter, and James; their spouses; and 18 delightful grandchildren who all encourage me to "go for it."

To my sisters, who are my very best friends and who always believe in me.

To all of my business pals and associates who helped me launch my business from just an idea that I used to talk about to really doing it.

To all the trusting clients who have allowed me into their lives to practice the art of Looking Damn Good.

To some special people who helped me bring my book to life: Angelique Devost, Claire O'Connor, and Tracy Ivie.

Thank you!

Table of Contents

Introduction
What You Might Like to Know About Me 1

Chapter 1
Looking DAMN Good: Appearance With Attitude 9

Chapter 2
Not-So-Basic Basics 25

Chapter 3
Getting a Lift With the Right Bra 39

Chapter 4
What Is Your Closet's Personality? 47

Chapter 5
10 Steps to a Reality Closet 51

Chapter 6
Your Amazing 10-Piece Wardrobe 61

Chapter 7
How to Shop: 7 Great Tips From the
Other Side of the Cash Register 65

Chapter 8
The Curative Powers of LDG 73

Chapter 9
The LDG 10-Step Remedy for Recovering From
All of Life's Traumas, Both Big and Small 81

Chapter 10
Professionally Speaking 85

Epilogue
Say "YES!" to Looking DAMN Good — and to LIFE! . . .97

Introduction

What You Might Like to Know About Me

My name is Janet Cargill and I am an image consultant. I get a kick out of hearing myself described as the "Fairy Godmother of Looking DAMN Good."

So how did I come to earn this designation, you ask?

An Education for Life at Salon de Beauté

I was raised by a very beautiful mother and a very handsome father. I know that because anyone and everyone that met them told me just how beautiful my mother was and how handsome my father was. When I was a very little girl, I did take note that when we went to the butcher shop in town, I always got a very large slice of baloney when I was with my mother. All the ladies I knew in town remarked about how handsome my father was, just in case I might not have noticed. When I reached my 13th birthday, somehow all my previous notions of growing up to look just like my mother vanished.

In fact, years later, when I was working at Liz Claiborne, I was helping a client, an elderly lady, who told me she was from Westfield, New Jersey. I always tried to find common ground with new clients, and so I said, "Oh, Westfield! That's my hometown. Perhaps you know my father, Mr. Leslie; he owned a beauty shop in town." She said, "Mister Leslie!? I was one of his regular clients. Why, he was the most handsome man I have ever known in person. And YOUR mother, why, SHE looked like a movie star!" Then, she paused, cocked her head to one side, and fixed a quizzical gaze upon me, as she remarked, "Why, you don't look a THING like either of them." The story of my life!

Both of my parents knew the importance to their business of always looking their best. I suppose I was genetically hardwired to know that my shoes, belt, and handbag had to match, along with being aware of the intrinsic value of a good haircut and the wonders of makeup.

My father had a very upscale beauty shop. My earliest recollections of his shop are the strong smell of permanent wave solution and nail polish remover, and the smell of clean towels from the laundry service. It was a fascinating place for a young girl to be. The manicurist tables had cute little scissors, bottles of nail polish in a rainbow of pinks and reds, and there were little funny-shaped dishes for soaking your nails — and chairs on wheels! My favorite was my father's big chair with the foot pedal that could make you go up and down.

Then there were the big floor brushes for sweeping up all the hair and the hairpins. No rollers or clips back then, just hairpins. My first real job was picking them up off the floor. I had a long broom handle with a magnet attached to the end. I would run my magnet through the cut hair and into the corners, under the chairs and anywhere a hairpin might be lurking. My goal was to see how many pins I could get before they fell off.

There were cotton balls for over your ears, and pink hair nets to cover the elaborate sets and to keep all the little curls in place while the ladies cooked under the noisy hair dryers while having their nails painted. There was the familiar cacophony of ladies' loud voices trying to chat with one another as they sat under the dryers with scissors snipping and snipping — all the rather wonderful chaos of the Salon de Beaute in action, with my father, the very handsome and charming Mr. Leslie, working the room like a maestro.

As I recall, all the ladies thought he was just wonderful. He could make any woman feel beautiful. Of course he had the required skills for haircuts, sets, perms, coloring, and the like, but his real gift was making each woman in his chair feel as if she was the most beautiful creature ever to set foot in his salon. I would watch my father work and be amazed at the transformation going on under his mindful ministrations. With the flick of his comb and a little poofing and puffing, Mr. Leslie would sell the lady on how gorgeous she looked. The women who went to my father's shop got their money's worth, and then some.

Retail Therapy

Fast forward many years. I'm in my sixties now and I've been married to my wonderful husband for 45 years. We have six grown children, three boys and three girls. Five of our children are married, and at last count (no one's called me this morning with news of another baby on the way), we have 18 gorgeous, healthy grandchildren. Much to our delight, all of our children are self-supporting, and still like each other — and us!

I was a stay-at-home mother for 30 years and did all the things that homemakers did, and loved it. Now I know that is a rather broad, sweeping statement. I admit, however, when you are looking back at life, the long view can often look like a wonderful collage of "Kodak moments." We all know that is not the whole truth. Some days were really hard. Some were endless and tedious. Some days I was totally out of my depth and felt like a complete failure as a mother and a wife. Many days I woke up and hit the floor running as if in a daze until I fell into bed at night. If I was lucky, I might even sleep until morning. When I do try to remember just what it was like, day in and day out, year after year, I can hardly believe it was really me living that life. Here is another amazing truth. The wonderful days and the hard, scary days are always lived in moments. Neither last for 24 hours, and one moment can follow quickly on the heels of the other in a flash! You know what I mean: at night just before you drop into bed, you tuck your precious little ones in just one more time, all cozy and sweet-smelling from their baths. You can't believe that you were at your wit's end just a few hours before and actually raised your voice in exasperation at those now (finally) sleeping little angels. From where I stand today I really mean that I DID love it. They were the most amazing and challenging days of my life and I don't regret one moment (now).

By the time I turned 50, some of our children were married and we were having grandchildren at a rapid rate. My mother-in-law moved in with us. My husband took early retirement from Bell Atlantic and began giving me "helpful" household hints such as how to load the dishwasher and do the laundry ("No need to separate the whites"). Generally speaking, I was the recipient of a running tutorial on how to improve most of my housekeeping skills. At the same time, I was getting a lot of phone calls that began with, "Hi Mom, what are you doing today?" Somehow I knew the next question would be, "Can you watch the baby (or babies) for me?" Don't get me wrong, I love my family, but the kitchen was getting crowded and I needed some time off.

One fateful day, I found myself at the Mall at Short Hills in the Liz Claiborne store, clothes shopping with a friend for her Alaskan vacation. Much to my surprise, the store manager asked me if I would like a job. She'd overheard me helping my friend and said I sounded like I knew what I was doing. Imagine that, a job with a paycheck with MY name on it, beautiful clothes at a discount, and a place to go to do two of my favorite things — dressing up and chatting — and get PAID for it!

It turned out that I not only had a natural talent for sales (which, after all, is what you have to do to try to get your kids to pick up their clothes and eat their green beans), but I also had a great eye for what each person looked good in. I had a flair for fit, style, and color. And because I had such a large family with lots of expenses (think orthodontia, times six), I knew how to dress well and look good with just a few well-chosen pieces. Even to this day, I don't have a lot of clothes, just a few of the right ones.

I spent the next ten years in the wonderful world of retail, dressing both men and women at Ralph Lauren, Brooks Brothers, and Liz Claiborne. I had lots of fun and also did some fashion show work. I developed wardrobe seminars and was called upon to do quite a bit of sales training along the way.

I loved my job and I loved helping people look their best. My very favorite part of the whole experience would come after working with a client who'd come into the store with a poor self-image who hated to shop, claiming she wasn't ever able to find anything she liked. My greatest payoff was being able to help her, and then have her look in the mirror with amazement on her face and say, "I never thought I could look this good!"

That's what I am all about. That's what I love to do and that's why I started J. Cargill Image Consulting. I believe every woman is beautiful, and my job is to help each of my clients see what I see.

You too can say, "WOW! I never knew I could look like this." Help is at hand. This little book is a compilation of a few priceless pearls of wisdom about Looking DAMN Good that I've gathered over the years working with women just like you. I am delighted to share them with you.

Here's to all of us Looking DAMN Good!

Cheers!

Janet

Chapter 1

Looking DAMN Good: Appearance with Attitude

The Origin of LDG (Looking DAMN Good)

There are so many adjectives in our language that one can choose to describe how a woman looks — positive, wonderful words like *lovely, fabulous, svelte, pretty, voluptuous, classic, feminine,* or *cute.* Cute — that's the word that was frequently chosen to describe me; I always really wanted to be described as stunning instead!

But no description of a woman had near the impact of my father's favorite description. My dad would come home from work and say to my mother, "I saw Lydia Brunner today; she looks damn good." I always wondered — what did that mean? The next time I saw Mrs. B., I would look at her quizzically as I tried to figure out just why she looked damn good. As I observed her — and other women who had earned my father's coveted LDG comment, I came to understand it was more about the way they *were* than how they looked. Yes, they were pretty — some more so than others, but it was more in the way they carried themselves, the sound of their voices, and the readiness of their smiles. It was about the total package. In retrospect, I can say it seems to me their insides matched their outsides. That's what the difference was. That's what mattered. That's what made them Look DAMN Good.

It took me years to come to an acceptance of my own LDG self. When I look back at old photos of myself, taken at a time when I still wanted to look and feel different than I was, I say to myself, "What were you thinking? You Looked DAMN Good!" Too bad I didn't know it then.

LDG isn't only for the special few. It is for everyone. It is an empowering way to feel about ourselves. When we know that and really "get it" — and by that I mean fully integrate it — it doesn't matter what we're wearing. We can then bring that empowerment to all the other women in our lives.

To quote Kathy, a recent LDG graduate, "Before we worked together, I thought paying too much attention to my image was a very superficial thing to do. You know, to be that concerned about the way you look.

I'd always pooh-poohed the idea as shallow. Then we worked together to get me ready for a big red carpet event at which I was to receive a major award. As I stepped up to the platform, decked out in the most beautiful red dress I had ever owned, my hair done up, my makeup just right — I felt like a queen. I KNEW I Looked Damn Good. I loved the way it made me feel. I felt confident, at ease, and focused. I know what I'm made of on the inside, and that pleases me. But I never had the feeling of my insides and outsides matching up. I want to feel that way all the time and let other woman know it's okay to Look Damn Good! It isn't shallow, it is empowering."

Don't Talk Fresh About Your Body — It's Listening!

We would never speak to a friend or loved one the way we speak to ourselves inside our heads and to each other. Even when we are paid a compliment, we are oh so quick to point out some negative aspect of our-selves (i.e. "you have lovely eyes," to which one might respond, "Well I guess so, but look at how big my thighs are.") Everything about us is too big, too heavy, too skinny, or too something. On and on we go with the disparaging remarks about our distressing body parts. Really, ladies, we are *not* a compilation of distressing body parts!

If you think it doesn't matter, let me tell you that it does. It matters a lot. Every thought we have shapes our cells, our bodies, our minds, and our lives. Think about how an infant would respond to that much negative input. As I listened to the ladies in the fitting rooms describe how they felt about their bodies, I started paying more attention to what I said about myself. It was an eye opener. I could see what a powerful negative impact those words had on my ladies as I realized the damaging effect they had on me. As I began working with women in the fitting room, I saw we were all essentially the same.

Before we ever got to the dressing room, we had an exhaustive list of everything that was wrong with us and how it must be hidden. Yet the women I saw had so many lovely features they didn't see. I never met a woman who wasn't beautiful, yet I seldom met a woman who believed she was.

The media has certainly played its part in shaping our self-image as women. In the 1940s and early 1950s, thin was not in, and yet I still managed to do a number on myself back then!

I would love to tell you how I quickly got the message — but old habits are hard to break. Sometime in my early sixties, I said to my longest and closest companion (me!), "You know you look pretty good for an old broad — as a matter of fact, you look really good."

My round belly had served me well; it had held eight children. I liked my "girls" (a.k.a. breasts); they were cute. I've cozied my children and grandchildren against them. I really liked how my hair was coming in salt-and-pepper. But it wasn't always that way.

The Plumpwear Balcony

The term *pleasingly plump* comes to mind to describe me when I was growing up. I bought my pleasingly plump little girl attire in a shop in Plainfield, New Jersey, called the Ideal Dress Shop. The pleasing — minus the plump — girls' dresses were on the main floor, nicely displayed with fetching combos already assembled. However, those of us who were more "pleasing" had to walk up a flight of creaky wooden stairs to the second level, where the "plumpwear," as I've come to call it, was located.

The plumpwear section was nothing like the main floor. It was nothing more than a balcony that served to hide the "less desirables" (clothing and girls) from the more "pleasing" young women on the main floor. It was basically plus sizes for pre-teens, with the ubiquitous elastic waistband and various features designed to camouflage.

Up in the plumpwear balcony, the lighting was bad, the selection was poor, and merchandise displays were nonexistent. There was absolutely nothing to indicate it was the kind of place an attractive young woman might like to shop. I still remember the humiliation of climbing those stairs, wishing I weren't quite so pleasing. Chubby sounded better; it indicated a certain cuteness and somewhat less permanent status. Voluptuous — now that's a wonderful word. It makes me think of the women painted by Rubens — lovely, curvy, soft, and feminine. But no matter how prettied up the terminology, anyone who bought their dresses on the second floor of the Ideal Dress Shop knew that plump was not pleasing.

Inner Adolescent Jet Lag

As a young girl, I was so invested in the negative aspects of my physical self that I barely noticed the changes taking place as I matured. I was unaware that I was growing into a beautiful young woman. Sadly, my unflattering internal self-portrait was the only one I could see. It makes me sad to look back and realize that I "missed" that part of my life and didn't even notice the lovely person that I can now see in photographs taken during those years. I am always just a little surprised when I realize that lovely young woman was really me. How come I never noticed? My self-image never caught up with itself — a sort of jet lag effect. My inner adolescent was still calling the shots. At the onset of puberty, the image that stares back at us in the mirror is really just a weigh station. The transformative lovely phase is just around the corner with marvelous changes to come.

As I've shared my story with countless women over the years, I have come to know so many other women like me. How sad to have wasted those precious years! I hated my "outsides" so much that my "insides" couldn't blossom either. The wonderful, beautiful young woman that was me had a hard time seeing the real person living in a unique body, perfectly designed to carry me through my life.

Most women are caught in a time warp, hanging onto the 13-year-old girl she sees in the mirror. She sits on her shoulder in the fitting room and whispers in her ear when she walks into a roomful of women. She's oblivious to the fact that most of the other beautiful women there are too preoccupied listening to the litany of their own inner 13-year-olds — that they're barely noticing the things you think are so awful and obvious about you, such as:

- Too fat
- Too thin
- Crooked teeth
- Frizzy hair
- Big breasts
- Flat chest
- Big belly
- Skinny legs
- Legs like tree trunks
- Football shoulders

It would be fun to walk around with cartoon balloons over our heads. Then we could all relax!

Interestingly enough, men are another story altogether. In all the years I worked in Brooks Brothers, never once did I hear a guy talk about his thighs or his waist. It always amazed me that a gentleman with a 48-inch waist, for example, would stand up on the tailor's platform in his slacks and announce, "Looks great, just mark 'em up!"

Looking Damn Good Is an Inside Job

When we talk fresh to our bodies, our spirits suffer as

well. Looking Damn Good starts on the inside, built from the positive, affirmative relationship we can have with our outsides. Let's choose new ways to speak about our bodies and the wonder and wholeness of who we are — words like: *Acceptance. Gratitude. Compassion. Awe. Tenderness. Joy. Respect. Inspiration. Sensuality. Beauty. Creativity.*

The way we relate to ourselves can either free us to be all we can be, or it can trap our spirits, our emotions, our pleasures, and our capacity to love and be loved. The choice is ours moment by moment.

Looking Damn Good is the vehicle that allows our insides to match up with our outsides. By respecting and talking nicely to our thighs, hips, breasts, legs, belly — whatever — we are affirming and loving who we are in the present moment.

We can be better stewards of our marvelous bodies. We can dress them becomingly, take good care of them, and want them to be healthy, active, and hang in with us until we don't need them anymore. When I got my most recent driver's license, the woman behind the counter asked if I wanted to be an organ donor, and I replied, "Well, sure! But I just want to let you know, I plan to use everything up by then."

Looking Damn Good is all about our insides and

outsides living together happily ever after. Once you know how, you'll never want to go back.

Treat Your Body Like You Would Treat a Good Friend

Whenever I speak to a group of women, I always ask them to tell me exactly what they don't like about themselves. Hands shoot up and the litany begins. Every one of my ladies is very clear about what they don't like and are not at all shy about sharing that information. Here are the top favorites that women have shared with me. My own personal favorites are listed in number one.

1. I hate my thighs, hips, and belly (this is the #1 group!)
2. I have a huge rear end
3. I have no backside
4. I hate my arms; they're too skinny, too wrinkled, too saggy, too fat, or too old-looking
5. I don't like my boobs: they're too big, too small, too droopy
6. I'm too tall/too short
7. I have bowlegs
8. My shoulders are like a halfback's
9. I'm too thin
10. I'm not a size 10 anymore

It is a very important step on your own LDG journey to write down everything that you don't like about yourself. You don't have to keep the list. As a matter of fact, it should be written on something that you can readily throw away. Please don't leave out this step. You will be surprised when you see the words and feel the impact those words have had on your spirit. I know I was. My own top complaint was that my belly was bigger than my backside. However, during menopause this can be true! I pictured all the fluffiness of my backside creeping around at night while I was sleeping and depositing said fluff on my unaware sleeping belly. The good news is that it is somewhat temporary. Let's face it, I'm not 25 anymore and neither is my belly.

Now comes the hard part. Make a list of everything that is really lovely and good about your body. What are your best assets? Go ahead, get started.

Are you having trouble thinking of even one? Most women do. Press on, though, because you MUST do this step. Everything else about Looking DAMN Good depends on making this list. Look at your body the way a dear friend might. Really look at your lovely neck and the beautiful curve of your full hips. Admire how your broad shoulders can carry off a layered look.

Here are a few more to get you started:

- Curvy, sensuous, soft hips

- Great backside (look good in pants)

- Generous bosom (also known as a good rack!)

- Perky breasts (not much sagging in your future)

- Lovely soft arms

- Great long legs

- Sweet, rounded belly

- Peaches and cream complexion

- Petite and cute

- Nicely proportioned

- Perfect nose

- Pretty hands

- Defined waist

- Strong back

- Sexy feet

- Full, healthy hair

- Broad shoulders (you can wear anything)

- Audrey Hepburn neck

- All the other lovely, beautiful features about your body that make you who you are

Now it's your turn! Don't skimp; find every little thing to admire, like you might imagine a big fan would. I suggest keeping this list in a place where you can see it. You should refer to it often. Habits are hard to break and some days we have a hard time remembering what it is that we like about our body. I know this to be true for me. I am tempted often to give my good old pal a hard time for looking wrinkled and a bit lumpy here and there until I realize once again that we have been hanging out together for 66 years. We've been through a lot. On a really good day, I can look at my good old self and be amazed at all the wonderful things we have done together. My body never failed to deliver the goods. She always cooperated in everything I called on her to do, from the time I was a little girl who ran like the wind through the waves that lapped against the sand at the shore, to dancing with my husband on our first real date, having wonderful sex, giving birth to many babies, scrubbing kitchen floors, sitting quietly knitting, reading into the wee hours of the morning, and jumping out of bed to take care of a sick child. Make your own list of wonderful things you and your incredible body have done together. You will have a new respect for her accomplishments and her ability to hang in with you day in and day out.

There are NO figure challenges that can't be enhanced. *It doesn't matter if you are a size 2 or a size 22. It is never about size, it is always about attitude.*

Whenever I think about that oft-used phrase of mine, I am reminded of...

The Red Teddy

One Saturday last spring I was with a few of my clients at my favorite bra shop, Personally Yours, in Bedminster, New Jersey. It is a tiny shop with only 2 curtained fitting rooms and it was quite busy — like Loehmann's on a big sale day. Ladies were trying on bras in every little nook they could find. We were all one big happy group having lots of fun together trying on bras and bathing suits as well. We did the "does this make me look fat?" routine more than once. In came another lovely lady to join in the fun. She was a large woman with an upbeat manner and she fit right in with the crowd. She asked the owner, Harriett, if she had a red lace teddy in her size, which was a 3X. She needed it for an anniversary cruise she and her husband had booked. Harriett handed her one in her size. The lady found a curtained-off spot to try on her teddy as she chatted about her upcoming cruise and how she always took something cute and sexy along for "play" to surprise her husband. The room fell silent as the voluptuous, lovely lady emerged from behind the curtain. She stood there as big as life, Mae West style, her head thrown back, hands on her hips and said a loud "Ta-dah!" We were all mesmerized. Almost on cue, we said as one "You look beautiful!" All 3X of her encased in red lace and bows. We laughed and applauded and knew we were sharing a marvelous aha! moment. Tears welled up in my eyes because I knew we were in the presence of someone who got what Looking Damn Good is all about.

It is never about size, it is always about attitude.

Chapter 2

Not-So-Basic Basics

Looking DAMN Good is about a polished look from head to toe, haircut to shoes.

Put Your Money Where Your Face Is

Your hair is a frame for your face. If you haven't changed your hairstyle in a few years, you can be pretty sure this is a good place to start. You know you have a good haircut if, two days before your next appointment, someone says to you, "I love your hair." Any stylist can make your cut look good in the shop with "products" and a good blow-dry. The real test of a good cut or style is in the growing-out stages; a really good haircut grows out well. To keep up with your cut, get in the habit of scheduling your next appointment before you even walk out the salon door. Women never like to break appointments with their obstetrician or with their hair stylists; some things are just sacred. In fact, it may be easier to leave your husband than it is to leave your hair stylist. Women almost feel like they have to move out of state to change stylists. You owe it to yourself to have a great hairdresser. Two bad cuts in a row, and they're out! Don't be shy in the checkout line if you see a woman with a great cut. Get out your notepad and tap her politely on the shoulder.

Makeup Is an Outfit for Your Face — Never Leave Home Without One

If you are unfamiliar with how to apply makeup, this tip is for you. Every department store has lots of cosmetic counters staffed with lovely women whose sole purpose is to teach you how to use their products to enhance your own beauty. They love it when you present yourself at their counter and say, "I am really not all that familiar with your products and how to use them. I would love to have you show me what I need and how to apply it." You are NOT obligated to make any purchases.

When choosing a cosmetic counter, look around and find a makeup artist whose makeup you like. She is the one for you. I've learned lots of interesting techniques and found shades of lipstick, eye shadow, and blush that were new to me that I might not have picked out on my own. It has been my experience that most of the makeup artists loved helping me. Sometimes I'd make a purchase if I REALLY loved the product. I repeat, you are under no obligation to buy, so please do not feel apologetic if you don't. Thank them and ask for their card so you can make any future purchases with them. Please do not hesitate in using this tip — and it's fun. You might want to bring a friend to share the experience with you.

My mother was the Michelangelo of makeup. My kids and I share how much fun it was to lie down at the foot of her bed and watch her makeup ritual. She took her time — my mother NEVER rushed, ever! It was truly a work of art. I have been ever so grateful to have learned the value of knowing how to "put my face on." Some mornings when I first look at my face in the mirror I think to myself, "In about a half an hour, I'm going to look a hell of a lot better than I do now."

You Don't Need a Lot of Clothes, Just a Few of the Right Ones

You don't need to buy a whole new wardrobe to change your look. However, you do need to purchase clothing that fits, looks good on your body type, and makes you feel lovely. Change the look with layering pieces, interesting jackets, and accessories. You should put most of your wardrobe dollars into some really good basics. Try working with what you have, using different combinations and accessories. Be very judicious when purchasing the latest trendy pieces. Think about the life expectancy of the garment — perhaps one or two items that are trendy and fun in a season is enough to keep you updated.

"Legal Skin" — What It Is and How to Use It

Legal skin is a term I use to set the standard of just how much skin (cleavage) we can show without getting a citation from the fashion police. I think a little mystery is always a safe bet.

Showing more skin around your face by using lower necklines, like a scoop neck or a boat neck, is a great way to "open up" your look – it creates a frame for your face. An open neckline tends to elongate the whole body. Think Audrey Hepburn. Rolling up your sleeves and wearing a skirt are two other ways to show more legal skin. It presents a more interesting look by creating a pattern of many different levels for our eyes to go to.

How to Take Inches Off Your Hips

This is one of my all-time favorite tips. It is so simple, yet the results are dramatic. Just by rolling up your sleeves your hips will look smaller — really!

Stand in front of a full-length mirror, both sleeves all the way down on your wrists. Look at your overall shape, especially your hip line. Then roll up just one sleeve and take a look at the difference between the two sides of your hip line. You will see a marked difference. When you roll up your sleeves your focus (and everyone else's) is no longer at your hip. You have created another level for your eyes to focus on by creating a different pattern. You can also wear a lovely bracelet or two for a more finished look. Seeing is believing.

Oh Where, Oh Where Has My Little Waist Gone?

Every woman has a waist. Somewhere along the line we seem to want to ignore that very vital space that actually creates the hourglass curve. "To tuck or not to tuck" becomes the question. In our zeal to hide our less than perfect waistline, we never show it; thus instead of a lovely curvy body we have created the box! There needs to be some indication of a waistline. Creating a focus on the waistline balances your shoulders and hips. This is another tip you have just got to try. Tuck in your top and put on a belt. This works best under a jacket or sweater for the more timid or short-waisted woman. Also you can put a belt on over a longer top, which is even more dramatic if you are wearing only one color. Wearing one color top and bottom creates a long, leaner line for the eye to follow. As a rule I only wear two colors at a time. My color column is either on the outside, jacket and slacks in the same color with my layering piece as the second color, or my color column is on the inside, with my layering piece and slacks in one color and my jacket or sweater in the second color.

Creating curves is about balance. If your shoulders are narrow, try putting a pin on the jacket next to the lapel instead of on the lapel. It extends the line of the shoulder outward, giving a broader look that balances out the hip line.

Fit Is It!

Knowing what is your best fit and recognizing what is the best silhouette for your body is the most important aspect of Looking damn Good in your clothes. Just as location, location, location are the three most important aspects of a good piece of real estate — fit, fit, fit are the three key elements of style.

Simply stated, clothing should fit well. Looking finished and pulled together is all about how things fit. That is much more important than price. You can pay a lot of money for a garment, but if it doesn't fit well, it will likely end up relegated to living on the hanger and you'll have wasted your hard-earned dollars.

We all have curves; let's make them work for us. Layering pieces should not be too baggy; they should hug the body. And please, no baggy bottoms. Too baggy is just as bad as too tight. Remember, you need to look good coming and going. Always check the "rear view" before you go out. Every dressing area should have good light and a full-length mirror.

Also, don't always go by the size that is marked on the item. You can wear a 12 in most things, sometimes a 10, or if the garment is quite expensive it could be a size 8. The more something costs, the smaller it is. Go figure. One of my clients refused to buy anything that was her real size, somehow the actual number appearing at the tag made her crazy — someone might see and figure out she really wasn't a size 4 after all. We solved that problem by cutting the tag out of everything she purchased BEFORE she left the store. She was happy; her "secret" was safe and her clothes actually fit. Whatever works for you.

Another problem can occur when buying different

colors of the same item. Take black, for instance. A pair of black slacks can fit you in a 12, but if you want them in white, you may need to get the next size up. Also, don't assume that if you're buying jeans and you want two pair — same size, color, and even the same style number — that both pair will fit the same. Try them on. Jeans are like snowflakes; there are no two alike. Trust me on this!

Try everything on. If you do, you won't have to do the return thing. Save yourself the hassle and try each item on. Murphy was an optimist — the one garment you don't try on *will* be the only one that doesn't fit.

Skirts and Slacks

A key factor in your appearance is the right length skirts and slacks. Slacks should never puddle on your foot – they'll make your legs look shorter. If you wear Petite, make sure your longer skirts are Petite as well; if you buy Missy or Regular, the proportion will be off. Business skirts have to fall just above the curve of your knee. Skirts that look fine while you are standing may be too short when you are sitting down, so be sure to check the fit while sitting down in front of a full-length mirror. You may be surprised where that hemline ends up!

Jackets

If the sleeves are too long, it'll look like you're wearing someone else's clothes. With a jacket, the critical fit is always at the shoulder. If the shoulders fit correctly, the jacket will hang well. Another fit issue with jackets is the waistline. It should hit at your natural waistline, not above or below. Even if you don't plan on buttoning a jacket, it needs to fit so that you can. The worst thing is to have a jacket too small; you will look bigger than you are. Remember, size is NOT as important as fit.

Tops

Layering pieces – which is what we'll call tops that are able to go under jackets or sweaters – should fit well and hug your body — especially if that piece will indeed be going under a jacket. Most women tend to purchase these layering pieces one size too large. If you do that, you'll hide your curves — and you want to see them. Just not too tight! You will see what I mean if you try on a smaller size under a jacket. The jacket should swing away from the body, which creates movement.

Necklines should vary, as well as sleeve lengths, colors, and textures. Choose both casual and dressy.

By changing your layering pieces with your basic slacks, skirts, and jacket, you can alter the whole look of an outfit, from casual to dressy, by changing only one piece. (More on this in Chapter 6, The Amazing 10-Piece Wardrobe.)

The Right Fabrics

Choose fabrics that are easy to care for and can be worn for at least three seasons. Look for clothes made from lightweight wools or poly-wool blends. Buy the best quality you can afford, as you can wear them over and over. Clothing made from rayon will wrinkle and is not user-friendly — it needs to be dry cleaned. Look for easy-care fabrics. No-iron cotton has risen to new and glorious heights in recent years. If you are now sending all your 100% cotton shirts to the cleaners what you are really doing is buying them at the store, handing them over to the dry cleaners (that phrase has always bothered me — the cleaning process isn't dry at all), and then proceeding to pay rent on them every week. It makes a lot more sense to invest in cottons that really are no-iron. The "ye olde cottage craft" of ironing needs to make a comeback. Knowing how to spruce up a wrinkled garment is well worth the effort.

One Shoe Does Not Fit All

The right shoe can make an outfit. The wrong shoe can spell disaster when trying to pull a look together. Less is more; your shoes should disappear off your foot, in a manner of speaking. Always check the look of a shoe in a full-length mirror.

Some of my ladies balk at wearing a pretty sandal type shoe with a dressy dress. I hear complaints that they can't walk in them. My response is always, "Get over it and learn how. If you learned how to be a lawyer or (fill in the blank), you can learn how to walk in pretty shoes." I'm all for comfort, but every once in a while I say, "No pain, no gain." Remember, Ginger Rogers danced the same moves as Fred Astaire, only backwards and in high heels.

A small heel is always a better choice than a flat; it does something lovely to your leg. Short ankle boots are a great choice with slacks in the cooler months. They can be worn with trouser socks, pantyhose not required. What's more, you can change the whole look of an entire outfit by simply changing the shoe.

Accessories 101 — The Power of the Pizzazz!

Skillful use of accessories can dramatically change any outfit. Be open to experiment with something different.

One really good belt with a great buckle is a must-have. Try to find one or two really interesting necklaces with coordinating earrings. If you're rolling up your sleeves, you may want a few bracelets and/or a lovely watch to decorate your wrists — a nice touch! Keep accessories simple but interesting. Experiment. This is another opportunity to ask the advice of a good sales-person. They are familiar with their merchandise and can offer some interesting suggestions. Remember, playing dress-up is fun. You don't own it until you've paid for it. I love getting input from the jewelry experts, as that is not my personal forte and I depend on good advice. I have changed my look dramatically with a few well-chosen pieces that I get a kick out of wearing.

Accessories have more of a punch when you choose just one terrific pizzazz piece, as long as the one you choose isn't a tiara!

"The Rule of Three" — Three Pieces Make an Outfit

This is a great rule of thumb. If you have on a top and bottom, your third piece could be one of the following: a jacket, a sweater, a great belt, a scarf, or a dynamite piece of jewelry. This third piece adds the finishing touch in a pulled-together look. It really is just that simple.

Wear Your Clothes With Attitude and Panache

Body language says it all. When you know you look good, pulled together and finished, your body responds. You walk tall, with more confidence. You look people in the eye. Your insides and outsides match. You have discovered how beautiful you are in your own unique, special way — and you KNOW it! You can now say it with me: "I don't just look good, I LOOK DAMN GOOD!"

Chapter 3

Get a Lift With the Right Bra

Nothing gives a woman more of a lift than the right bra. The right bra can take years — and pounds — off your figure. It instantly does away with that "dumpy feeling." You wouldn't want to build your house on a bad foundation; the same holds true for your wardrobe!

Bras are one of THE most important pieces of clothing a woman can purchase. A properly fitted bra makes all the difference in the appearance of everything you wear. A lousy bra can make an expensive designer outfit look awful. I know many ladies who would balk at investing in a good, well–fitting bra because of the cost, who then go on to buy other pieces that are much more expensive and not nearly as important and essential, like handbags. Believe me, a great-looking bustline is worth way more than an expensive handbag.

My First Bra

Getting my first bra was a moment that is forever burned into my memory. When the day came, I think it was long overdue. We went on a mission to the lingerie shop in town, The Corset Shop, owned by Mr. and Mrs. Klein.

Back in the day, there was no such thing as a training bra. I've often wondered, "What are they getting trained for, the Olympics?" My mother took me — and my untrained boobs — to visit the Kleins on East Broad Street in Westfield, New Jersey. The memory makes me queasy. Mrs. Klein wore sensible, rubber-soled shoes and a tidy bun. Mr. Klein wore suspenders and a cloth tape measure draped around his neck. They seemed very old to me.

The shop wasn't trendy or cool. It was a shop dedicated to getting down to business. It was like going to the dentist, only worse. At the dentist, all you had to do was open your mouth. But in the barely-curtained cubby on East Broad Street, you had to expose your untrained breasts to be measured, assessed, and viewed by both Mrs. Klein and my mother. I tried to keep Mr. Klein in my line of vision at all times, worried he might peek.

Mrs. Klein had shelves and shelves of long boxes

with all sorts of mysterious garments, that, fortunately, I wasn't "ready" for. I went home with an assortment of sensible bras that I would "grow into". No sense getting one that actually fit, my size might change. They were made of a serviceable, stiff cotton, with lots of stitching in a circular pattern all over the cup. When you placed your untrained breasts into the cup, they became a pointed arrangement, the sole purpose of which was to stand at attention and not move.

What I didn't appreciate then and what I have ultimately come to realize is that the Kleins were experts. They knew exactly what shape and size bra you needed. They knew what was in all those boxes. No little hangers, no huge assortment of styles. No baffling arrangements of straps.

Making Peace With Our Breasts

It is an interesting relationship we women have with our breasts, myself included. I have inverted nipples; in case you don't know what they are, suffice it to say I could be at the North Pole in a T-shirt and nothing would show. That's the good part. I had always thought I was somehow deformed and felt very self-conscious. I never wanted anyone to see my nipplelessness except for Mrs. Klein, my mother, and my sisters, so no one else saw my "deformity."

That seems like a strong word for something so simple, yet that is how my 13-year-old self felt about my breasts. Looking back over the years, I can see how damaging my negative, limiting body image really was. It reached into all the areas of my developing self. I felt less than, not as good as, set apart... I was flawed in some intrinsic manner. Slightly imperfect. You can buy clothing items like that on the bargain racks. What I didn't see was that my body was wonderfully and perfectly made for me!

I had an aha! moment on a retreat last May. I was attending the Creativity Spa workshop with Jennifer Louden and Camile Maureen at the Laurel Springs Ranch — a beautiful spot high atop the mountains overlooking the coast of Santa Barbara, California. I spent 7 days with 19 amazing women of all ages. The younger ones among us loved to swim in the buff as well as enjoy the wonderful experience of soaking in the hot tub under the starlit skies in their birthday suits. In a moment of delicious abandonment, I stripped my 65-year-old, somewhat lumpy, nippleless self down to the raw and jumped in. What a wonderful gift I gave myself in that moment. I was finally free of that haunting feeling that I carried deep within the recesses of my mind that I was somehow flawed, and not as good as everyone else. As I got out of the water one of the young lovelies said, "Janet, you have the most beautiful breasts I have ever seen." I love my "girls" today and they are truly beautiful.

I am not alone — we women have all sorts of odd ideas regarding that part of our anatomy. In my work over the years, I have helped other women as well as myself come to have a friendly relationship with our breasts. Never, ever speak ill about the "girls." They can't help how they were made.

I have seen many, many others besides mine and I will tell you that they are all quite different. As far as I can tell, there is no standard. Small-breasted women bemoan their smallness; large-breasted women bemoan their bigness. We need to make peace with what we have. Accept them. They have been with us, if we have been fortunate enough to keep one or both of them, since they first bloomed. Develop a friendly, caring relationship with your breasts. Put them into lovely bras that show them off to their best advantage. Make sure they are comfortable and well-supported, like you would support your best friend.

The Holy Grail of the Perfect Bra

In my years in the fitting room, I was always amazed at the array of women in bras that didn't fit. We all know that gravity is a force to be reckoned with, and if you don't support those puppies when you're young, your 36B will turn into a 36 Long. I think it's easier to choose a wedding gown than it is to pick out a decent bra. Why is it so hard to go bra shopping? You find a department, find your size, and away you go, totally uplifted. Right?

Well, it's not so easy, is it? First, there are those silly little hangers, and the tags — oh my! The tags alone can make you crazy. And then there's the dizzying variety. What kind do you want? Soft cup? Underwire? Racer back? Strapless? Padded? Unpadded? What kind of padding, the stuff that mattresses are made of, or the kind that gets dents?

After you've decided on the type, now you go and look for your size. Most likely, it's the one size they are out of. Ugh. Back to the drawing board. Some bras are more like hammocks for your breasts — a sling type deal where they rest comfortably and hang out — much like you would on a hot summer's day. Some fit and feel like a suit of armor. They take your breasts up very high, strapping 'em in where they threaten to jump out of your blouse at any moment. Then there's the bra that causes the "Uni-boob" to emerge. It is a rather uninteresting arrangement that travels across your chest from armpit to armpit.

Bra shopping is an enormously daunting task. The choices are overwhelming and the information is totally inadequate. I think that's why so many — I would say MOST — women are wearing the wrong size bra. There is hope. Bras are finally coming into their own as the pivotal piece of clothing they truly are. Now, thank heavens, in this modern day, there are endless possibilities for the arrangement of your breasts. And there are, if you are fortunate enough to have one in your area, Bra Ladies. Seek one out and become her groupie. You simply cannot Look damn Good without the right bra.

Bra Tips:

- The bra should feel quite comfortable — no pinching, tugging, or straining.
- If underwire, the wire should lie flat against the ribs and sternum — a.k.a. breastbone — between the breasts; no floating or hovering underwires.
- At the side of the underwire, all breast tissue should be in front of the wire, not smooshed under it in any way.

- Avoid the dreaded spillover effect, especially the less firm and nubile among us.
- The straps are not in charge of lifting the breast. That is the job of the body of the bra. The bra should stay in place and be supportive even if the straps fall down.
- When new, the bra should do its job clasped on the first or loosest, row of hooks, not the tightest.
- You get what you pay for; don't expect to Look damn Good in a $15 bra.
- Never machine wash your bras, not even on the delicate cycle. Hand wash after every second wearing. I know this may seem like a pain, but this important practice keeps the fabric from losing its body, as oils from the body cause the elastic to deteriorate in fairly short order. Use a mild detergent or a baking soda product, such as Forever New. Rinse twice and always drip dry. Heat from the dryer deteriorates the elastic even faster than body oils.

Chapter 4

What Is Your Closet's Personality?

Do you have a walk-in closet that you would rather run away from?

Do you have a closet full of clothes with nothing to wear? Do you ever think, "I'd love to have a new look but I don't know where to begin?" Do you feel that everything in your closet looks the same, making you feel boring? Do you stand and stare into the abyss that is your closet, filled with clothes from days gone by? Do you have clothes that have shrunk just by virtue of hanging there for the past several years?

Getting honest and admitting you have a problem is the first step to change! Admit that you are powerless over your clothes and that your closet has become unmanageable.

Here's a list of the major closet types that I've either had myself or that I've worked in. Do you recognize yours?

The "I Can't Throw Anything Away" Closet
a.k.a. The "What If?" Closet

This is the most popular type of closet. Hangers are jammed and tangled. There's no breathing space at all. Clothes are trapped in there that haven't seen the light of day in years. The owner of this closet hasn't any real idea of exactly what's in there because she's afraid to look. These are the most fun closets in which to work because there are so many treasures to uncover, most of which the owner has completely forgotten about.

The "Past Lives" Closet
a.k.a. The "Memory Lane" Closet

In this type of closet, lots of space is gobbled up by garments whose function is more relevant to whom the owner USED to be than who she is today. I have taken tours of these closets with their owners and have gazed at clothes that have not been worn in 15 to 20 years. It's a veritable walk down memory lane, filled with fond – or worse yet — NOT-so-fond memories of long-ago events. 99.9% of these clothes will absolutely never be worn again and they're clogging up the works.

The "All Sizes" Closet
a.k.a. the "Yesterday and Tomorrow" Closet

These closets consist of clothes from yesterday and, it

is hoped, for tomorrow, but not much for today. There is always hope that tomorrow I may fit into yesterday's clothing. Let it go. I promise, it's okay. The you of today is just dynamite; invite and embrace this truth.

The "I Always Buy on Sale" Closet
a.k.a. The "Closet for Orphaned Clothes"

This closet is filled with clothes purchased while in the mindset: "I don't really need this and I don't have anything to go with it, BUT it was on its third mark-down and I just couldn't pass it up because it was such a steal." These orphans have no relationship whatsoever to one another and seldom have anything to match.

The Malnourished Closet
a.k.a. The "I Hate to Shop" Closet

This one needs an emergency transfusion of new clothes. When looking into this type of closet, I always wonder what the owner managed to find to wear yesterday. P.S. If this describes your closet, you can skip Chapter 5 Steps 1 through 8 and go directly to Step 9.

10 Steps to a Reality Closet

I've come up with 10 steps that will give you a Reality Closet. What is a Reality Closet? It's one that is filled with clothes that you love to wear, that look good on you, and fit your unique body type. It includes appropriate wear for a wide variety of occasions, along with the right shoes and accessories. A Reality Closet is a pleasure to walk into and choose the outfit of the day. It feels as if you are going shopping in your own highly personalized boutique.

This is the exact same process I use when I work with my private clients. They all love the results. You can do this process alone or with a girlfriend – a Reality Closet Buddy — and take turns helping each other!

1. Set aside a large block of time.

Make sure you give yourself plenty of time. Note: It WILL take longer than you think. And it's discouraging to get only halfway through, and if you stop, it's even harder to get started again.

2. **Have the items that you will need on hand.**

   - Plastic or wooden dress hangers

   - Clip hangers for skirts and slacks

   - Shoe racks or hanging shoes bags

   - Large plastic storage bags for out-of-season clothing

   - Large bags for clothes that you will be donating

   - Full-length mirror

3. **Put on your best and prettiest undergarments.**
   This step is vital for moral support as you will be spending a good deal of time looking at yourself in a full-length mirror. Also, the clothes you try on will look better with the right underpinnings. (See Chapter 3.)

4. **Take out all the clothes that you love to wear and feel good in FIRST.**
   Try each of them on and take a good look at yourself in the mirror. See if you can discern why you like these pieces. What appeals to you most?

Check out the necklines, proportions and balance, sleeve length, and fabric type. Where does the jacket fall on your hip? Does it fall at a good length above or below the widest part of your hips? Are the slacks the right length, not too short or too long? How does the seat look?

This step is critical. We all have some lovely things in our closets that make us feel good when we wear them. It's important to look at all the elements outlined above. When culled from the pack of clothes that you may not love, there will likely be a common thread in terms of color, style, and fit. Take some notes.

The most important thing will be that you feel GOOD in these clothes. These slacks, jackets, blouses, shirts, and dresses are going to be used as a starting point, a template of sorts, against which to gauge the rest of the things in your closet and the new items that you will purchase.

5. **Start the sorting process.**

For some of us, this is a very difficult step. If you can't contemplate doing this part of the process by yourself, invite a trusted friend to help you decide what to keep and what to recycle from your closet. Most of us would do well with some moral support. The sorting process needs to include shoes, handbags, and outerwear as well. An important part of this process is deciding where you are going to donate all the lovely things that no longer work for you. It is an excellent idea to have a list of places that want your good clothing. Look for women's shelters, "Dress for Success" shops, and the like. I have found that women are more eager to part with things they can no longer use but are still in good condition if I introduce them to the "New Lady." That's the lady they haven't met from one of these organizations who is just waiting to have those lovely clothes to wear that will give her a whole new life. It is important that we keep these "New Ladies" in mind when we are tempted to hang on to items that may just languish in our closets gathering dust and taking up valuable real estate. It really feels good to watch the pile grow higher for the new ladies.

Take everything out.
Get down to the walls, carpet, and rod. I had a fun experience with one of my delightful ladies. She

was reluctant to go the distance and take everything out. It had been a long-neglected closet and it really needed a good cleaning out, like my refrigerator. Much to her dismay, I kept saying, "Keep going, you're almost finished." She reached for the last shoe that was in the very back corner of her closet. It had long ago lost its original shape and looked like a dusty fossil from another age. Her hard work was rewarded — under that shoe was a beautiful gold bracelet that she thought she had lost forever many years ago. Perseverance pays. Who knows what you might find?

Outdated?

This category includes your poodle skirt, a jacket better suited for Joan Crawford, and that miniskirt you wore back in the 1960s. You get the idea. If you're waiting for an outdated fashion to come back, remember, styles come around every 30 years. Determine where your garment is on that timeline. Chances are you'd do best to let it go in order to make room for something fresh and delightful. And as a woman of a certain age (like me), one (ahem) might not have another 30 years to wait.

Old, tired, worn, nubby, and/or faded?

Be ruthless with this category. You may want to keep a few pieces from this group for working in the yard or painting. Or some of them may be good old pals that are just plain comfortable. I call these clothes "infits," not to be confused with outfits. Infits never leave home like outfits do. Choose some of your favorites and put them back; they've earned their place.

Items you've never worn?

There's usually a good reason why you haven't worn them. Perhaps they don't make you feel good. Try them on and in a moment you will remember why. Let them go.

Multiples of the same items?

I once saw a stack of sweatshirts numbering at least 30, all neatly folded. Determine the maximum number of sweatshirts — or whatever your "thing" is — that one can reasonably wear. Allow for how often you do in fact wear them, and how often you do laundry. Then fill someone else's need with your leftovers.

If you've done all the steps thus far and everything has been looked at, tried on, categorized, and/or set aside for someone else, you're now ready to move on to the final steps where you'll get to see the payoff for all the sorting, trying on, and tough decision-making.

6. **Choose which pieces earn their way back into your closet.**

   This is what to put back into your closet: all the great things you love to wear; those funky pieces that you don't yet know what to do with; and all the skirts, slacks, and tops that fit well, even if you haven't found anything to go with them yet — in short, anything that looks great and is still in style and in good shape. NOTE: Avoid the temptation to put back anything from your discarded piles. However, for the faint-hearted, you have my permission to choose a few of these items, but you must first wait 24 hours.

7. **Hang up in an orderly fashion.**

   Here's a quick lesson in Hanging 101: separate jackets from their bottoms. Hang similar items together, like with like — skirts with skirts, jacket with jackets, and so on. I love to hang clothes in a closet the same way you see them hanging in a clothing store, from short to long, light to dark. Put seldom-used pieces in the back, such as formal wear or special occasion pieces that are not part of your everyday working closet.

8. **Stand back and take a look.**

Look at all the things in your closet and use your imagination. Play around with pairing that skirt with that funky jacket that you didn't know what to do with. See if there are color or texture combos you haven't tried before. Get creative and play dress-up with these lovely clothes. Try out different combinations. When your clothes are hung in such an orderly fashion, it feels as if you are shopping in a boutique, not your closet. You'll see everything with new eyes.

9. **Make a "Wants and Needs" list.**

Prepare a shopping list for the items that you still need or items that you really would love to have — like a special leather jacket or a great pair of boots. Make sure you have the items that are necessary to make outfits from what you already own. What is your wardrobe missing? A little black dress? Some new slacks? Different layering pieces? How is your shoe inventory? Think about what you need that you don't have. There are some great tips on how to shop in Chapter 7.

10. Celebrate!

Congratulations! Now, give yourself a pat on the back for a job well done. Most of my ladies feel like a new person after this process. Some say they feel 20 pounds lighter; it's incredibly freeing and energizing. So stand back and look at your lovely Reality Closet filled with only the things that make you feel and Look Damn Good!

Now, have a lovely cup of tea and relax — you've earned it!

Chapter 6

Your Amazing 10-Piece Wardrobe

Creativity is the mother of invention for a small budget. You don't need a lot of clothes, just a few of the right ones. It works for me. I've taught hundreds of women how to accomplish a great wardrobe starting with 10 easy pieces. I've run into customers from Liz Claiborne years later who are still getting maximum mileage from 10-piece wardrobes I helped them construct many moons ago.

As you know, before I was in business, I was an at-home mom for 30 years raising six children — think pediatricians, braces, Christmas presents, bikes, sneakers, and so on. Now, multiply by six – and all on one income. You get the picture. Not too much left at the end of the month for clothes for Mom.

As a result, I learned very early on to make each purchase count. If I currently had one good pair of black shoes for that season, I didn't buy anything brown. Each carefully chosen piece had to multi-task. I once had, in my dowdy days, a bathing suit with a skirt. More than once, I was tempted to put on some pearls and heels and wear it to church. Well, not really; the skirt wasn't long enough!

Furthermore, every single thing I bought had to EARN its way into my closet. People always say to me, "You always look so nice, you must have a lot of clothes." I just smile and say, "Thank you!" Clients and friends are surprised to know I don't have lots of clothes; I find that having too many garments is overwhelming and confusing. Also, having fewer clothes enables me to have some play on the hanging rod, which is essential for organized, efficient – and fun – dressing in the morning.

Also, what they don't realize is that I just keep changing my combo. All of my clothes are mix and match. I have a color scheme that works for me and some wonderful basic pieces. I just change my layering pieces, jackets, and accessories. I still make new combos that surprise even me! Less has always been more for me. It's all in the art of the combo.

With your 10-Piece Wardrobe, you should be able to mix and match and interchange all of them with each other to make at the very least 25 different combinations! Use your imagination, your accessories, shoes, belts, and handbags. You'll be amazed at what you can come up with that are well beyond the 25 that are the no-brainers.

Here are the ingredients for your Amazing 10-Piece Wardrobe:

Pieces 1, 2, and 3 — A Jacket, Skirt, and Slacks

These are your three basics, around which everything else is built. Have them in the same fabric and solid color. They should be rather classic and neutral. Brown, black, gray, or navy, whichever is your best color.

Piece 4 — A Second Jacket/Blazer

Pick a jacket that has some texture, perhaps tweed, velvet, or some other fabric that has some color and that offers a nice contrast to your three basics.

Piece 5 — A Second Pair of Slacks

If your second jacket is a pattern, have this second pair of slacks be a solid. If your second jacket is a textured solid, such as velvet, your second pair of slacks could be tweed or a solid. Another great choice here is an outfit jean. Choose a dark wash with a tailored look. These jeans are versatile enough and might be worn to some offices on Casual Friday.

Piece 6 — A Third, Softer Jacket

Examples: a chunky sweater or even a well-cut denim jacket that would work over all the bottoms and give a casual laid-back look to your basics. I love a good denim jacket!

Pieces 7, 8, 9, and 10 — Four Tops

These layering pieces are key. You can have fun with them and really let your personality and mood show. These pieces should have very different looks. Casual and dressy. Scoop necks, turtlenecks, square necks. Choose pretty colors that frame your face. And remember, don't be afraid to show some legal skin!

Most importantly – and here's where it all comes together — make sure that ALL the tops go with ALL the bottoms and go under ALL the jackets.

Chapter 7

How to Shop: 7 Great Tips From the Other Side of the Cash Register

Let me tell you what an excellent adventure I had in the wonderful world of retail. Each day, as I stepped through the doors of Liz Claiborne, all the busy-ness and the normal chaos of my household world fell away as "Miss Janet," as I was called, appeared — calm, focused, and full of energy and enthusiasm. My days sped by.

The busier I was, the more I enjoyed it. A typical busy day went something like this: The fitting rooms were full. Salesladies were darting in and out with more lovely clothes for the ladies to try on. There was lots of laughter and chatting going on — oohs and aahs — as one woman after another discovered her LDG self looking back at her in the 3-way mirror. It was sort of like the lunch scene from "When Harry Met Sally" — heads would pop out from behind the fitting room curtains and ladies would say, "Give me all the clothes that she's getting — in my size."

Brooks Brothers came along with an employment opportunity I couldn't refuse. When I was leaving Liz for my new gig, I was amazed to learn that I was the top-selling agent in the country for Liz Claiborne. Who knew? I had come directly from my kitchen!

My first few days at Brooks Brothers were rather intimidating, very somber and quiet. There were lots of dark suits with sizes I didn't know about quite yet. I was not only the new kid on the block, I was a woman from Liz who had come with a reputation as being an excellent salesperson. I had to prove myself. What did I know about menswear? I felt out of my depth for a few days — the whole tie thing just got to me. I didn't have a clue at first as to what tie went with what shirt and suit. Then it hit me! Ties were the third piece, like scarves are for women. I was off and running. I soon became known as the Queen of the Tie Bar — my male counterparts started asking *me* for help. It wasn't long before I earned the respect of the sales staff and the tailors as well. They all taught me well. The guys at Brooks Brothers called me "Turbo Shoes" because I was good at what I did AND I was fast!

What I learned from my time at Brooks Brother

and Liz Claiborne, as well as Ralph Lauren, provided me with a wonderful education for my own business. I could not have gotten better training elsewhere.

So many women dread the idea of shopping. It can be confusing and overwhelming, to say the least. Here are some really good tips for how to shop and actually get what you went to the mall for.

Tip #1 — Always shop with a list.

It is really important to know what you want. If you have done Step 9 of your Reality Closet exercise, you will have your list at the ready in your handbag.

Tip #2 — Have a destination in mind.

Know what stores work for you in terms of style and budget. You may have to spend some time getting to know where the clothes live that you love and that look good on you. This will keep you from wandering aimlessly about and getting discouraged.

Tip #3 — Know your weaknesses.

If you are an owner of an Orphan Closet or the "I got it on sale" closet, I am talking to you. BEWARE the 70% Off sale rack and the third and final markdown racks. I know how intoxicating and alluring those signs can be. But before you run to the cash register with your booty, stop and THINK, "Do I really NEED this? Or am I buying it only because it was 70% off?" That is the question. The answer separates the veteran sales shopper who only buys what she really wants or needs, and the impulse sale shopper who buys it only because it's 70% off. My mother was famous for quite often bringing clothes home for us that mostly never fit and weren't anything we wanted or needed. When we protested, she shot back her standard remark, "I HAD to buy them; they were so cheap I couldn't just leave them in the store!" That made sense — how? I remember a Christmas present I got when I was 20 years old. It was a white rabbit fur muff. Can you imagine how I felt was when I opened that gift? It had come fifteen years too late. I would have enjoyed having that when I was five to go with my velvet trimmed Sunday coat. But at 20? It must have been at least 70% off.

Tip #4 — Pick out a good salesperson.

When you enter a store, look around to find a salesperson that looks somewhat busy. Don't choose the ones that are leaning on the displays and chatting with co-workers. The salesperson who is busy and moving usually is the best at what she does. Look for someone who has a smile in her eyes and a cheerful greeting. She is a good one to start with.

Tip #5 — When the question is "May I help you?" the answer should be "Yes!"

Tell the salesperson just what you are looking for and where you'll be wearing this piece, and give your size. Give her as much information as you can. That way, she will have a clearer picture right off the bat and will be eager to help you. If she doesn't have just what you want, ask her if she can suggest something else that may fit the bill.

Here's the thing: she should know where everything lives in the store, what goes with what size or style, and what she has in the stockroom. If you're buying more than one or two items, tell her that; she'll prepare a fitting room for you and be thinking of what else she might bring you that's on your list.

What so many people do is walk into a shop and when approached by a salesperson they try to hide in the racks alone and say, "I don't need any help." YES, YOU DO! Most good salespeople really want to help you. I could always spot a customer that needed me but was fearful of getting an overly aggressive salesperson. My approach was always a casual, friendly "Hello, how are you?" that often led to me gently making some suggestions that she could choose from. An excellent sales associate has so much information that can make your shopping so much easier.

Even though I am a very experienced shopper, I ALWAYS ask for help and am vocally appreciative of really good help when I get it.

When you find good sales help in your favorite shop, you have arrived!

Tip #6 — Ask about coupons, special offers, or dis-counts.

When you get to the cash register, ask if there are any coupons that are being offered. Even if you don't have one, most good salespeople will give you one to use if they have it available. If you're spend-ing a large sum of money and they say you can get a 10% discount if you open a store charge, you might want to think about opening and using it just for that purchase. Then pay it off right away; store cards usually have a high interest rate.

Tip #7 — When in doubt, pay by credit card.

When you're not sure about an item, or if you want to live on the edge and purchase something you haven't tried on first, check the store's return policy. When in doubt, don't pay cash. Credit cards are easy on and easy off. Cash and checks get complicated.

Chapter 8

The Curative Powers of LDG

It is a scientific fact, probably even discussed in *The American Journal of Medicine!* When a woman is recovering from an illness or surgery, doctors and nurses know she's "turned a corner" when they hear this telltale request: she asks for her comb, lipstick, and a mirror.

I know this to be true from my own life. When faced with illness, trauma, and other awful stuff, including "I am SO having a really bad day," I reach into my tool box for the utensils that will get me through. I've had some wonderful role models as a child and throughout my life — really strong women — responding with grace and authenticity to their own difficult moments. I've discovered the common theme, "When the going gets tough, the tough put their face on."

The Best Part of Getting Sick

Of my earliest memories of illness, what sticks out is

not the awful, tortured, feverish stuff. Instead, what I remember very well is what happened AFTER the fever broke. THIS was the best part.

My mother would help me out of bed. I was all shaky-legged and sweaty and smelly, with my fur-coated teeth and severe bedhead. My body was a charming medley of various odors: Vicks Vapo-Rub® on my chest, Robitussin® breath, and, if it had been a "heavy chest," there was also the aroma of my mother's mustard plaster concoction.

I was now ready for the most curative procedure of all.

The bed was stripped, replaced by fresh, white sheets and pillowcases (contents puffed and plumped). The nightstand was cleared of little piles of wadded handkerchiefs, half-empty glasses of stale ginger ale, and spoons crusted with red cough syrup.

I would go, oh so willingly, into the bathroom to brush my teeth and take a short wonderful bath. I was permitted to use some of my mother's good talcum powder. I then brushed my hair into submission and donned a clean nightgown. These were some of my very first LDG moments.

I will never forget that wonderful feeling of my clean, powdery-smelling self as I slipped into the sheets that had the aroma of the outdoors. Everything around me was tidy and peaceful. I still might've felt less than 100%, but it was hard to top this blissful part of the recovery process. It was the part that made it possible to even consider being able to go back to school again. If I close my eyes, I can still feel and smell the wonder of it all. I know I can tap this resource whenever I need it.

The Cherry Red Present

There is a level of unspoken knowing among women that binds us together.

I was not quite 23. I had a 10-month-old daughter when I gave birth to premature twin boys. It had been an extremely difficult labor and delivery, during which I was close to losing my own life. My babies only lived for a few hours. I heard them cry, but I never had the chance to hold them, to kiss them, and to say goodbye. I was devastated, emotionally spent, and physically depleted. It was difficult to find any sort of peace or closure. Words could not penetrate the profound sense of loss and grief I felt.

When my husband arrived at the hospital to bring me home, he had in his hands a beautifully wrapped gift from my mom with just the words, "Love, Mother" on the tag. I opened the box, and tucked into the crisp, white tissue paper was a beautiful cherry red wool skirt with a soft sweater in the same pretty red. I took the outfit out of the box and tears welled up in my eyes, as I felt a tiny little space open in my tightly closed, sad heart.

My mother, being of Irish descent, wasn't an openly affectionate woman. We came from the stiff-upper-lip regions of the world, but as I ran my hands over the soft sweater, I knew what her gift to me really was. It was her way of telling me that even though I couldn't change what had happened, couldn't bring my little babies back, couldn't change what was – I could put on my cherry red outfit, comb my hair, wash my face, put my lipstick on, and pick up the threads of my life. My cherry red outfit was a symbol for me that no matter what might happen, I could always find a way to reach inside and call forth some thread of resilience, to cope, to move forward, even to thrive – with grace and poise. That was 43 years ago. I have never forgotten my twin sons, or my cherry red skirt and sweater.

It was a timely message for me. I couldn't have known the many challenges that I was yet to have in my life. Raising six children was at times a daunting task. Staying married through it all was no piece of cake, either. I remember those times when I would say to myself after some unpleasant exchange or another with my husband, Bruce, "I am SO out of here! If he thinks he can (fill in the blank), then he has another thing coming. I'm as good as gone!" Then I would realize all the diapers were still in the dryer and one of the kids had a dentist appointment after school. And, I still had to make dinner. Fast forward and somehow we've made it 45 years. And I'm glad.

Lipstick and Meatloaf

This is the story of another time when lipstick AND meatloaf for dinner changed the course of my life in an instant.

I was 40. The youngest of my children was 3, my oldest was 19. It had been a difficult run of a few years. My husband was finally recovering from a long-term illness that had exhausted both of us and taxed our children. I had been feeling pretty poorly for a long while, and after months of tests and doctors' visits, my doctor sat us down in her office and gave us more difficult news. I was diagnosed with sclero-derma, a disabling and life-threatening auto-immune disease. It was progressing rapidly and I was to become more and more disabled. Some of the more painful aspects of the syndrome could be held at bay for a while with strong steroid drugs, but life as I knew it would never be the same.

We both sat there, stunned. This couldn't be real. But it was. I cried and cried all the way home. How was I going to manage? It was already so hard now; how could I possibly cope as the illness progressed? I was at the bottom of my ability to function. I considered throwing myself out of the car onto Route 22. Perhaps I would "fall" under a bus.

Then, the faintest, tiniest wisp of a thought came into my mind. I had defrosted two pounds of ground beef that morning. It was Monday — we often had meatloaf on Mondays. It would be close to dinnertime when we got home, and the kids would be hungry. They were used to me pulling up my socks and taking care of things during their father's long illness; it helped them feel safe. I didn't want them to feel scared seeing my tears. It always makes things way worse if the kids get upset as well. So, I made a decision. I wouldn't jump out of the car and end it all. Instead, I would dry my eyes, comb my hair, put on my lipstick, and go home and make meatloaf. Twenty-five years later, I am still here, and I'm still making my meatloaf.

Now, there was more to my recovery than making meatloaf, but I am absolutely sure that single, small decision to pick up the threads of my life yet once more, to "keep on keeping on" was the most important decision I was to make in dealing with my own illness.

When faced with a "meatloaf moment" in your own life, try using the 3 Cs: Cry, Commit, and Continue.

CRY: Have a good cry. You really need to do this. If you want, go ahead and think about jumping under the bus, then:

COMMIT: Be still and wait for that little wisp of a thought that will come to you, the thing that you need in order to get up and get back on your own road, and then:

CONTINUE: Pick up the threads and the tiny pieces of your life. Take one small step forward. We have so many wonderful mundane tools all around us for helping us to move on: laundry to be done; ground meat to defrost; lunches to pack; soccer games and choir practice to chauffeur; dinner to make; a job to do. These are the things for which I am ever so grateful. This is the blessed stuff of our lives that pulls us forward.

Remember, "When the going gets tough, the tough put their face on."

Meat loaf recipe available upon request.

Chapter 9

The LDG 10-Step Remedy for Recovering From All of Life's Traumas, Both Big and Small

After a challenging time in your life, when you feel ready to begin again, here are the 10 sure-fire steps to put you back into action.

1. Take a warm, soothing bath. Not the quick shower-and-go, but a relaxing bath with some lovely potions that will make your skin soft with an aroma that brings a feeling of relaxation, such as lavender. A relaxing bath helps drain the tension from an aching body that has been under prolonged stress. Just sit and soak.

2. When you feel like a prune, get out and dry off. Then slather (don't you love that word?!) yourself with a rich moisturizing body lotion. Use a very gentle hand, like you would with a small child.

3. Moisturize your face using a loving touch.

4. Dress yourself in something that makes you feel beautiful. What quality are you going to need today to get going? If you need fast energy, choose a bold color. If you still feel fragile and tenuous, a soft color and fabric is good. (Pink is wonderful.) If you have been very sad and need to feel a little lighter again, choose yellow, any yellow — it's a happy color. If you have been ragged and raw, choose something blue. It will help you feel calm and serene.

5. Fix your hair. Take time with it, until it feels right.

6. Put on your VERY BEST FACE. Check the dark circles under your eye and use your concealer. Don't use a dark eye shadow today; a bright, open eye is best.

7. Watch what you eat. Take time with your meals, focus on good wholesome foods, drink lots of water, and don't have too much sugar. Have a lovely cup of tea in a real china cup.

8. Turn on some music that makes your heart sing.

9. Read something that lifts your spirits. One of my favorites is any little chapter in Anne Morrow Lindbergh's book *A Gift from the Sea.*

10. Thank God for all the wonderful blessings that you have in your life.

This LDG Prescription comes with a Misery-Back Guarantee. If you don't feel better, you get your misery back. No questions asked.

Chapter 10

Professionally Speaking

You never get a second chance to make a first impression. You are your best business card and your sharpest marketing tool. You need to make the RIGHT impression the first time and every time.

I open all of my business professional seminars with the statement above. Before I say anything else, I ask this question of my audience: "What do you know about me already?" The feedback I get from the groups is always the jumping-off point for me to hammer home what I know is obvious. What I look like, how I am dressed, how I carry myself, my posture, the way I move about the room, the timbre of my voice, where am I directing my gaze, has already given my participants volumes of information. They have made many assumptions about me both positive and negative. My goal when I take the stage is to project confidence and an easy, open attitude that puts people at ease, and to broadcast the one very important piece of information that people will "get" right away — that I am SUCCESSFUL! That is the single most important message that you want to send to your prospective clients. In the business world, appearance always counts!

If you work for a corporation, it is just as imperative to present well. You represent the company wherever you go. You carry their image with you. You want to be the one in the meeting that sets the bar higher. Your CEOs are watching and will appreciate your taking the time and energy to present the company image in such a professional way.

Years ago when my husband and I were very young, we received an invitation to an event that promised that we would become extremely financially successful if we participated in marketing a line of beauty products. I thought it sounded wonderful. Earn extra money and still be able to stay home with the kids. You know — easy money, a win/win situation. We sat and listened to story after story about how much money these folks were making. It sounded very compelling and lots of the audience members signed on the dotted line. Before my husband weighed in with his opinion, I said, "This is a crock." We didn't know anything about pyramid marketing at all; it was still a very new concept. But I DID know one thing: If I made that much money, I would look a hell of lot better than these people did. It may sound a bit shallow, but it is still true. When you are trying to sell your skills or your product, you must look like you are doing well NOW! No matter what the presenters told me, after making my own observations, their comments fell short. The company did go belly-up not too many years later. It is important to look successful as you make your first impression, but that alone will only get people to have an immediate positive response. You still need to know what you are doing and be able to deliver the goods.

There are three important factors for being successful in any business endeavor:

1. Passion
2. Expertise
3. Presentation

All three must be present. You can't balance on a two-legged stool. I have had personal experience of my own trying to balance on a two-legged stool. I spent some time as a Realtor working for a wonderful agency. I was encouraged to make the move to real estate by one of my clients at Brooks Brothers who admired my sales skills and made a wonderful pitch to join his company. Now I loved selling clothing and making people look and feel Damn Good, but soon realized that selling a house was not the same as selling a suit.

When someone walked into Brooks Brothers and asked me for a navy suit, I would pull one out in the correct size, we would go into the tailoring area, and expert tailors marked it up. I would add some shirts and ties and perhaps a belt and socks. Easy as pie. Not so with folks buying a home. We would go through the looking for the house of their dreams, just as they described it to me. After many phone calls and lots of driving we would get to the house that I was sure was their "navy blue suit." As we walked through I could hear myself chatting away, with just a touch of too much perkiness, describing how it fit all of their specifications. I would hear in my head the words that all Realtors long to hear: "I'll take it!" But alas and alack, quite often their comment was along these lines — "Well, I don't know. The kitchen is a bit small." Nitpicking, thought me. Now mind you, I loved to sell, but I soon realized that I loved to sell clothing, and I was not good at selling houses. I looked very professional and very successful. I had gotten my license (I thought I would die during the state exam). I had taken the agency's course as well and had learned how to use a computer. I loved chatting on the phone. I had some expertise, but I was not passionate about the job. I couldn't get balanced on my two-legged stool, so I danced back to the wonderful world of retail and left the business of selling homes to the real estate professionals who loved their work.

Presentation:

I am an expert image consultant and personal stylist, and I am passionate about the importance of people presenting their best selves. Now that is a topic that I can sink my teeth into. Speaking of sinking your teeth into something, meatloaf comes to mind again.

In defining Presentation for you, I like to draw on my real-life experience. I have a great meatloaf recipe, and I am passionate about cooking said meatloaf. But it was always necessary to present it well to my family. Some were not as passionate as I about another meatloaf for dinner. So here's the deal:

Presentation! Never serve meatloaf on a paper plate with a slice of Wonder bread. I always presented meatloaf on a lovely platter with a bit of parsley for flair. Hot brown-and-serve dinner rolls and mashed potatoes with really good gravy sealed the deal.

Same meatloaf; different response. When you are in a business or working at a job where everyone has the ability to gain the knowledge and expertise, they all have the meatloaf recipe. Some will also be passionate about their work. What will be the very thing that might separate you from the pack? PRESENTATION. You can be the meatloaf on the good china plate.

Years ago, when Ward Cleaver went to work, dressing for the office was easy. He wore a suit and a tie. IF Mrs. Cleaver did work she knew exactly what to wear. Women in the workplace had very definite and strict guidelines. All you have to do is think of the job and you get a very clear mental picture of what those guidelines were. Nurses wore white, nuns wore black, secretaries from Katie Gibbs wore gloves, stockings, and sensible shoes with a small heel. There was very little guesswork when it came to what to wear to work.

Things have changed, the workplace has changed, what is acceptable and professional attire has changed. We can be more creative in how we dress. The graphic artist, the writer, the jewelry maker, any profession that deals in the arts should dress in such a way that they are able to express their unique creativity. No navy blue suit here, please. The banker and the financial consultant need to look like they have done very well for themselves and will do a good job handling your money. Never give your money to an investment broker who looks shabby!

In the preceding chapters you will find all the information that you might need on how to build a dynamite wardrobe for business using the tips in Chapter 2, "You don't need a lot of clothes, just a few of the right ones."

Also, remember it is ALWAYS about fit, even more than price. If you are starting out in your professional life, spend your money on the pieces that you need to last a long time. Suits, jackets, blazers, a few good pairs of shoes. These are investment pieces. Count them as a business expense. However, and let me be clear on this point, you do not have to spend a small fortune to get started. Choose wisely and make sure you get the best possible fit. You may spend only $199.00 on a suit, but don't balk at the alteration fee. That's what makes an inexpensive suit look like you paid much more. You can buy the expensive stuff when you get the big paycheck. When you do get the big paycheck, make sure it looks like you did. A good professional wardrobe is a sound business investment. I have known people who will spend lots of money on brochures, stationery, business cards, and so on but not much on their most valuable business asset — themselves.

People DO notice the small stuff. That's what separates the wheat from the chaff.

Too much is always too much. Too much perfume, after shave lotion, jewelry. Leave the navel rings at home. Underwear should stay "under." Shoes should always be polished. Do you know what color shoe is best to wear with navy? If you guessed black, you would be wrong. Cordovan or a deep burgundy is best. Your belt and shoes should always match.

For the Gentlemen

I've included tips for the men here as well, even though my little book is intended for women. Hopefully, you can use this information if the man in your life WANTS input. That is the key. Lots of guys won't ask for help with their clothing. They would rather bumble along thinking it really doesn't matter what they look like, instead of asking for help. It's like when they drive around lost, but refuse to ask for directions. Another clue as to who needs help is the guy who comes to you ready to go off to work or wherever and asks, "Do these two greens match?" The answer to that question is always "NO."

Here are some good tips for those guys who need them.

Men, make sure your neck size is not too big; you should be able to tuck your thumb in the neck. Shirt sleeves should not be too long. Know if you are a regular, long, or short in a suit. If you don't know, ask. If no one knows, use this tip: If the sleeves of the jacket need to be shortened more than an inch and the jacket looks a tad long and it's a regular, try on a short. Also, if you asked for a regular and you look like Ichabod Crane, try on a long. Your suit jacket should bisect your body — equal amount of leg to upper body. If your pants are too long, your legs will look short.

You know you have the right size belt when there are two holes on either side of where the pin goes in. Make sure you always try the belt on with the pants you'll wear with it. Belts that are marked the same size are not always the same length.

Socks matter! There should be no skin showing when you cross your legs. Socks can have interesting patterns as long as they go with your suit and shoes. Ties make a statement. You can get creative and expressive. A fun tie in the right circumstances is a good icebreaker ("Hey, great tie!"). One of my clients always wears wild ties with his conservative suits and jackets. We decided to forego the Hawaiian shirts in favor of the fun ties. He isn't sorry. They have become his trademark. If the tie looks like it is too inexpensive, go up a notch. Cheap ties are a dead giveaway. Choose ones that lie nicely and have some oomph! Learn how to make a really good knot. You can look like you've lost weight and inches off your midsection by making sure the tip of your tie covers your belt buckle. This is another one of those simple yet very effective tricks.

Casual button-down shirts don't go with a suit. Save them for sports jackets and blazers.

When in doubt, remember that good taste is always the right choice. Good grooming is always appropriate. Even men need to check their fingernails. I call it a finished look from haircut to shoe polish.

For the Ladies

For my ladies, legal skin is the rule. Also, remember

to notice where your skirt winds up when you sit down! Check necklines by bending over in front of a mirror. You might be surprised. It is the small things in life and in business that are important.

The very best thing to put on each day is confidence and enthusiasm — it shows in your smile, your voice, and your eyes. Walk with confidence, head up, tail tucked under, and know that you look good, you feel good, and you are good at what you do — and as a matter of record — You Look and Feel Damn Good! Go for it!

Epilogue

Say "YES!" to Looking DAMN Good – and to LIFE!

I hope you decide...

To say YES! to feeling and being beautiful and empowered.

To say YES! to moving out of your comfort zone.

To say YES! to living your life dressed in your "best self."

To say YES! to having confidence, polish, and style.

To say YES! to ridding yourself of clothes — and everything else — that no longer work for you, or fit your new insight of who you truly are.

To say YES! to being part of the solution of helping others find their own Damn Good Selves.

I know from my own struggle to accept my LDG self how hard it is to say that first small yes to loving and accepting myself just as I am. Of course, saying yes means dealing with all the internal voices of my doubts and fears. My psyche would rather throw up some convenient road block than to really feel how uncomfortable I am moving along my own path. It can feel quite scary at times — or sometimes just plain silly.

Life always brings us lessons. We can choose to be open. We can choose to listen. We can choose to turn away. We can also choose to say "Yes," even if it's a small yes at first.

Our family rented a cottage for a few weeks this past summer down the shore, on Long Beach Island.

We were fortunate that so many of our children and grandchildren were able to come down and stay with us. It was a time spent filled with so many of my favorite things — showering outdoors, big steaming pots of sweet corn, sleepy babies under the beach umbrella, mounds of sleeping bags and wet beach towels all around, quiet conversations on the porch, listening to the melody of voices and the laughter around the supper table, cooking with my kids with all hands on deck, building sand castles at the water's edge, finding FIVE whole moon shells, and watching the sandpipers dance with the waves. There was so much magic that each day felt like one long Kodak moment!

Lest you think it was all pink roses, it also happened to be the hottest week in August — you could feel the weight of the air pressing on your skin, cloying and thick. There was an unrelenting land breeze that lasted for six days. In case you did not know this, a land breeze down the shore brings the biting flies. So, now we have oppressive sticky air peppered with biting flies. To top it off, the water temperature was really cold, so it was tough to get the relief one might normally hope to find down the shore.

There were a few brave souls in the water. Or maybe they were nuts, I'm not sure. Much to my continuing amazement, it seems children are unaffected by the cold ocean water. I do recall from my own childhood being much more intrepid in this regard.

Here's the scenario: I'm standing at the water's edge, dodging sneaky waves and slapping at the flies and two of my granddaughters, Mary Kate and Janet, ages 10 and 11, are bugging me to go into the water with them. Both of these girls have earned Ph.D.s in the "Art of Bugging" and were using their A+ material on me.

Now, I have had this exact same conversation, verbatim, innumerable times at the water's edge with my own children. Many years ago, I came to the rather adult conclusion that I don't like going in the water much anymore. Plug in the excuse of the hour here — because it's too cold, too rough, I'm relaxing, I've just eaten, I don't feel like it, I'll go later, or my all-time favorite, I don't want to get my hair wet.

To wit, my granddaughters kept up the well-practiced offensive, "Puh-leez, Grandma, so what about all of that?!" "JUST DO IT!" "YOU NEVER GO IN THE WATER!"

Then, a strange thing happened. As I stood there, considering my usual litany of excuses I had just uttered, I realized it was all just a crock! I was so used to saying all of those words, I really hadn't thought about them much anymore.

I don't really understand what happened next. I heard my voice saying, "YES! Let's go!" I took their hands and we ran into the freezing water, screaming and shouting, "WA-HOO!" Then, the most marvelous, wondrous thing happened. I LOVED it. The water was freezing, but it was absolutely delicious. I had never felt anything quite like the exhilarating feel of that icy cold water all over my body after the muggy discomfort of the last six days. It made me feel alive, excited, renewed, and amazed all at the same time. My astonished family stood dumfounded at the water's edge. The ones back at the blanket trickled down to the water and, stupefied, asked their dad, "What happened to Mom?"

What happened to Mom was that in spite of my time-worn, well-rehearsed objections and my locked-in behaviors and ideas of why it was impossible for me to run like a child into the freezing water, my body decided to say "YES!" to the invitation and jump in. My spirit responded in the most extraordinary manner, feeling delight in that awesome moment when I experienced the icy delicious water freeing me from me. It was a moment that won't soon be forgotten.

So, I invite each of you, my dear readers, to say YES! to the invitation to jump into your beautiful selves and live your life, Looking and Feeling Damn Good!

J. Cargill Image Consulting
Look DAMN Good!

About Janet Cargill

A highly sought-after image consultant and motivational speaker, Janet is a seasoned traveler in the world of fashion — and meatloaf.

She is equally skilled working with the president of a major corporation as with a young teenage girl, struggling to find a sense of style along with her way in the world.

She's spent more than 16 years as a wardrobe consultant, fashion show coordinator, and executive sales trainer for Brooks Brothers, Ralph Lauren, and Liz Claiborne. A mother of six children and 18 grandchildren, Janet has been married for 45 years.

How to Contact Janet

For information on a private image consultation, Janet's current seminar schedule, or to book her for a speaking engagement:

Janet Cargill

J. Cargill Image Consulting

902 Fox Hill Court

Milford, NJ 08848

Web: www.jcargillimage.com

Email: janet@jcargillimage.com

Phone: (908) 310-2148

FREE eNewsletter

Subscribe to Janet's eNewsletter, "On Fashion, Food, Family & Fun." It's entertaining and informative, full of real-world tips delivered with Janet's trademark humor and wisdom.

Simply send an email to janet@jcargillimage.com with "Subscribe me" in the subject line.

A Note to Meeting Planners

Janet loves to share her enthusiasm for the transformational power of "Looking DAMN Good." A natural public speaker, Janet leaves her audiences inspired, moved to tears, laughing out loud — and wanting more. Her trademark humor and down-to-earth wisdom has won her devoted fans from all walks of life. She speaks to a wide range of audiences from corporate to support staffs to community and educational groups. She offers keynotes, workshops, and all-day or weekend retreats.

Partial List of Clients:

Smith Barney

Morgan Stanley

Coldwell Banker

Prudential Realtors

Rutgers School of Business

Professional Meeting Planners Association,
    New York City

Hunterdon County Chamber of Commerce

National Association of Women Business Owners

New Jersey Association of Women Business Owners

Call or email for booking enquiry or meeting planner packet.

Phone: (908) 310-2148

Email: janet@jcargillimage.com

Praise for Janet and the Effectiveness of LDG

"The difference in my closet is like night and day. I finally had permission to throw away things I hadn't worn in years, things that didn't look good on me and things that were worn and tired. I discovered some lost treasures I had forgotten I had and put together outfits with things I had that I never would have thought to put together. After my closet was finished (in one day!!), I had more outfits to wear than ever before, with much less clothes and not spending one penny on anything new!

It's effortless to get dressed in the morning. It's simple to find everything, it's organized. I wish I had done this years ago. I spend much less on clothes than I ever did. Even though I'm not quite the size I want to be, I feel better about the way I look and the way I feel about myself than I ever did. When Janet and I go shopping I spend much less money and don't feel overwhelmed, as I used to. I've learned to mix and match and to shop without spending a small fortune! Thank you! Thank you! Thank you!

Before, I felt anxious, scared and very nervous – I also felt extremely vulnerable. After, I felt weary, but great. I was surprised by how many combinations of things I already owned. I also felt very safe within five minutes of our being together. I loved the mix and match ideas and learning why certain things looked good on me. I also loved the idea that things must "earn" a home in my closet. I've learned to wear all my clothes – not to save everything for special occasions. In addition, I learned it's important to me to look "good" every day for myself.

You are really onto something here, Janet! You are very good at what you do. God has blessed you with a special gift. I'm delighted you've chosen to share it with me.

— Eileen M.

"...Even more importantly, you unwittingly lifted me spiritually to a place I haven't been in some time, which allows me to operate at an entirely different level. This, of course, has a positive affect on my over-all mental attitude and improves performance both on the job and in my daily life! It's hard to put into words, but your ability to discover and highlight one's "positive points" is transformational. You gave me so many gifts today. Well, look out world – the door has been unlocked and who knows what lies ahead because you found the key! I am looking forward to a long and lasting team effort to create the person that I want to be.

— Colleen L.

"My girlfriend's husband asked me if I lost a lot of weight. I had been told that I am "glowing" and that I look like a "goddess".

Here I am almost nine months after my makeover and I am still receiving compliments: I love your hair, you should keep it that way; I like your outfit, you look like you're losing weight; that eye shadow really compliments your skin color.

My special day had a profound effect on my self-esteem and self-image. I'm still the same person but I am totally different, transformed and ecstatically happy. There are very few people who have a profound effect on our lives, but the time I spend with Janet changed my life forever.

— Cathy K.

"I thought I knew everything there was to know about fashion and then I met Janet! Janet reintroduced me to my wardrobe and reinvented me with MY own clothing! And I received tons of compliments on my 'new outfits.' Janet redefines expert. This woman knows her stuff and you will leave her presence knowing you look like a million dollars!"

— Shannon W.

Patty Zeller —

Care giver ?

CPSIA information can be obtained at www.ICGtesting.com
Printed in the USA
BVOW05s1612200215

388669BV00001B/1/P

9 781434 321787